Contents

Safety note:
Please ask an adult to help you
when making bubbles.

Getting started

Bubbles float in the sink.
Bubbles pop in a glass
of lemonade. Mix together
simple ingredients and make
your own super bubbles.

What you need:

4 L
warm water

240 mL
washing-up liquid

15 mL
glycerin

large plastic
bowl

spoon

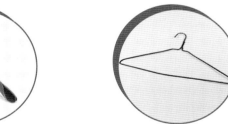

wire coat hanger

drinking straw, potato masher,
spatula or other utensils
with holes

pipe cleaners

Making bubbles

Pour 4 litres of warm water
into a large plastic bowl.

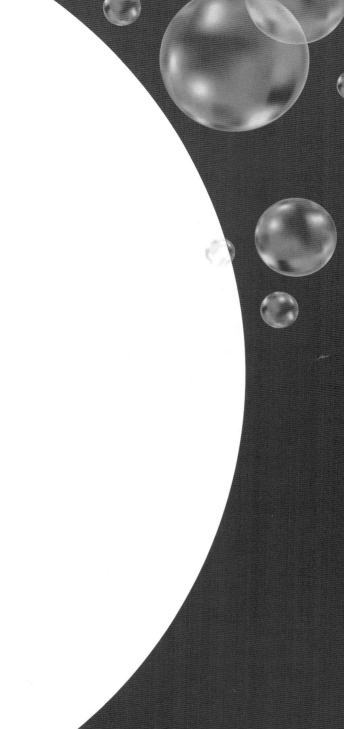

Add 240 millilitres of washing-up liquid.

Next, add 15 millilitres of glycerin.

Slowly stir the mixture.

Try not to make
too much lather.

Let the bubble mixture sit
for two or three days.

Make your own bubble wand
by shaping a wire hanger
into a circle.

Wrap pipe cleaners
around the hanger.

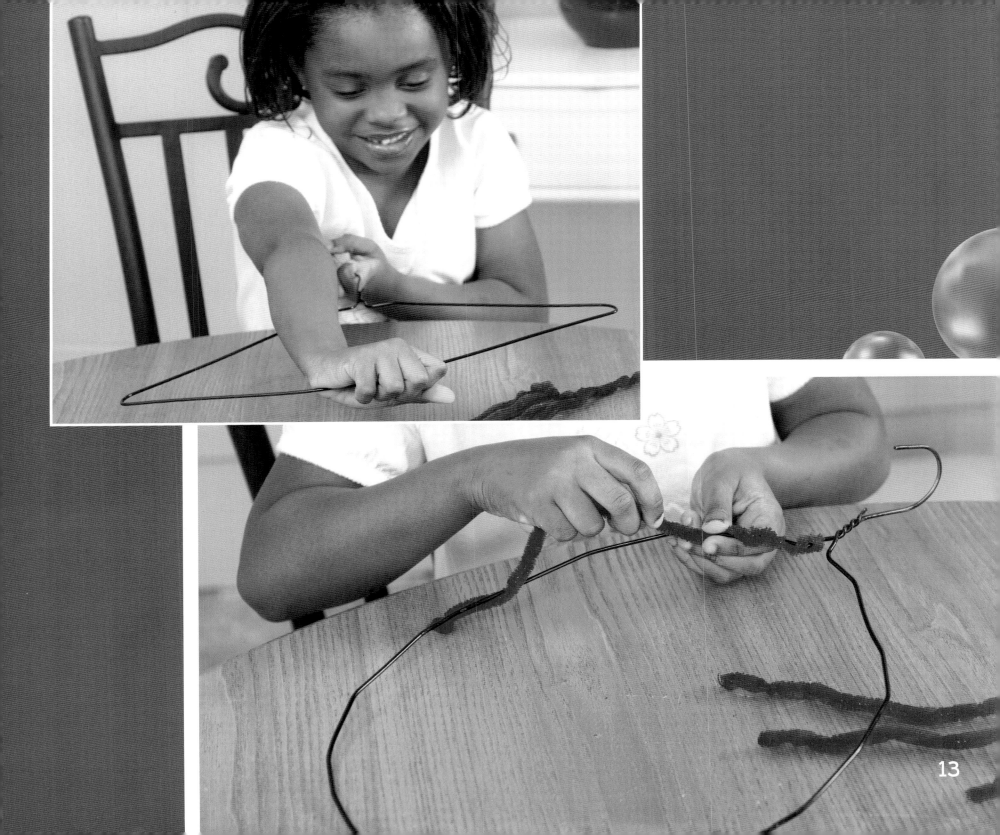

Ask an adult to carry

the bowl outside.

Blow lots of bubbles with a straw.

Dip a potato masher into the bowl.

Blow through the holes.

Put the hanger into the mixture.

Pull it out slowly. Gently move it through the air.

You may have to try several times before you make a giant bubble.

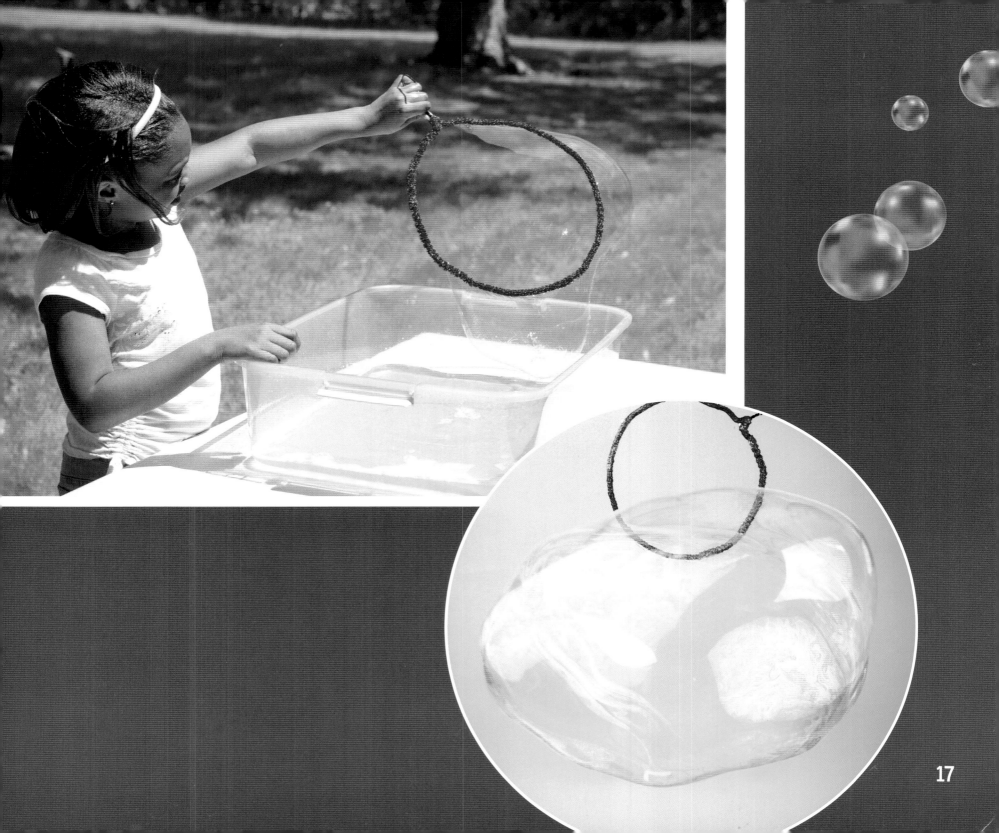

How does it work?

Blowing air can make a thin film of soap stretch. When stretched too far, the film snaps closed. Air trapped inside makes a round bubble.

Bubbles burst when they dry out.
The soapy film gets too thin
and the air inside escapes.
A bubble also breaks when
it touches something dry.

Glossary

burst   break apart suddenly

escape   get away from

film   very thin layer of something

glycerin   syrupy liquid used in soaps, perfumes and other products

ingredient   item used to make something else

mixture   something made up of different things mixed together

Read more

Experiments in Material and Matter with Toys and Everyday Stuff (Fun Everyday Science Activities), Natalie Rompella (Raintree, 2015)

Materials (Real Size Science), Melanie Waldron (Raintree, 2014)

Science (Jobs If You Like…), Charlotte Guillain (Raintree, 2013)

Websites

www.bbc.co.uk/terrificscientific/curations/z22qtv4
Explore and contribute to real scientific investigations on the BBC's Terrific Science website.

www.bigeyedowl.co.uk/science/index.htm
Ideas to encourage and extend scientific skills.

www.science-sparks.com/category/early-years-science-2/sensorymessy-play/
More fun activity ideas to help investigate core science concepts.

Comprehension questions

1. What happens when a thin film of soap is stretched too far?

2. What can cause bubbles to break?

3. What other items do you think you could use to make bubbles with your bubble mixture?

Index